African Magic Series

SEVEN AFRICAN POWERS
THE ORISHAS

MONIQUE JOINER SIEDLAK

Oshun
Publications

Other Books in the Series

African Spirituality Beliefs and Practices
Hoodoo

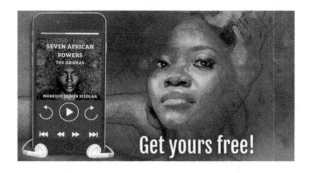
Get yours free!

Want to learn about African Magic, Wicca, or even Reiki while cleaning your home, exercising, or driving to work? I know it's tough these days to simply find the time to relax and curl up with a good book. This is why I'm delighted to share that I have books available in audiobook format.

Best of all, you can get the audiobook version of this book or any other book by me for free as part of a 30-day Audible trial.

Members get free audiobooks every month and exclusive discounts. It's an excellent way to explore and determine if audiobook learning works for you.

If you're not satisfied, you can cancel anytime within the trial period. You won't be charged, and you can still keep your book. To choose your free audiobook, visit:

www.mojosiedlak.com/free-audiobooks

WANT UPDATES,
FREEBIES & GIVEAWAYS?!
MONIQUE JOINER SIEDLAK
THE
ORISHAS
JOIN MY
NEWSLETTER!
mojosiedlak.com/newsletter-signup

Contents

Introduction   xi

1. Yoruba   1
2. Elegua   7
3. Yemaya   11
4. Oshun   15
5. Chango   19
6. Obatala   23
7. Ogun   25
8. Oya   29
9. Spells   33
10. Orishas in the Home   53
11. Orishas Days Through The Week   55

Conclusion   57
References   59
About the Author   61
Other Books by Monique Joiner Siedlak   63
Please Review   65

Introduction

The Seven African Powers are seven of the most well-recognized and celebrated deities of the Yoruban culture. Also identified as the Orishas, they are common to all beliefs of the Yoruban starting position, while they are not always considered to be the same deities. In Vodun, they are perceived as Loas or Lwas. In the Macumba traditions, of Candomble and Umbanda, they are called Orixa. While in Santeria, Voodoo's corresponding religion, they are spoken of as Las Sietes Potencias and lastly, in the Congo Basin, they are referred to as Nkisi.

The Orishas are claimed to be the emissaries of Olodumare. Olodumare is a gender-neutral, divine, all-knowing and deity who created the earth and the entire universe. The Orishas are demi-Gods who have been assigned to watch after mankind. They oversee the forces of nature in addition to our troubles.

The Orishas recognize each other and are seen primarily by their distinctive numbers, colors, markings, meals, and personalities. These dictate what gifts and contributions are acceptable for each Orisha. The advocates of all the Orishas will require contributions in the way of which they are used to so that the Orishas acknowledge correctly and will provide an answer in the presence of a spell or curse. Understanding the forces of nature that guide them, the Orishas can be best known by. For example, Elegua is located at the crossroads, while Oshun enjoys the rivers and streams.

A secure relationship with that one dominant spirit influence provides an individual to request for the aid of all seven spirits in every undertaking. The Seven African Powers are called upon for overcoming obstacles; help with spiritual change, and encouragement of personal power. Any individual can call upon the Seven African Powers bearing in mind that they are spirit guides and anybody, whether they are initiated or not, have contact with spirits of the deceased for their direction. Normally they are called for by burning a vigil candle, which is seven colors or using seven different candles to represent the various colors. As you call the Seven African Powers and petition them for help, fasten strips of scarves or fabric of seven different colors in a bundle and spin in the air above your head.

Collectively, these seven Orishas symbolize a force that offers guidance and strength during the course of all our troubles and hardships.

ONE

Yoruba

Archeological evidence shows that the Yoruba people became a notable presence in the West African world sometime around the 5th century B.C. The founding father of the Yoruba people was King Oduduwa. He resided in the capital city Ile-Ife, which, to this day, is considered to be a sacred symbol of the Yoruba people. Some old stories present Oduduwa as a creator deity, making Ile-Ife the place where humanity was created. But historical accounts speak of battles for supremacy against unruly invaders.

Prior to Oduduwa, the Yoruba were a scattered nation, living in semi-independent cities ruled by chiefs (*obas*). The twenty-something cities had twenty-something kings, who had their own subordinates to keep the villages in check. So, we can't speak of a united nation. The only key element that identified them as "Yoruba" was their language.

Once Oduduwa became king, the Yoruba kingdom was born. The role of the king gained importance, and the kings that succeeded him called themselves "the sons of Oduduwa." It also became customary for people who desired influential political roles to prove their lineage as descendants of Oduduwa. After Oduduwa's death, his sons moved from Ile-

Ife to start their own kingdoms. Twenty-five new kingdoms arose, all centralized and all recognizing Ile-Ife as the primordial city. All these kingdoms led to the existence of distinct Yoruba subgroups, each with their own variations on religion, language, society, and politics. Some important Yoruba kingdoms were Oyo and Ekiti (in the northwest), Owo (in the southeast), and Awori and Shabe (in the southwest). King Oni of Ife and King Alaafin of Oyo are, to this day, celebrated as great Yoruba kings.

The modern Yoruba culture was born as a result of a battle for power, which led to a great conflict and a fragile reconciliation, as shown in their myths and stories. This constant battle also plagues the more recent history of the Yoruba. The wars for slaves weakened the kingdoms. Yoruba slaves were sent to European colonies in the new world where white men would never accept their religion. Yet, their traditions and beliefs survived. How? The clever Yoruba people practiced their religion under the veil of Catholicism. Both religions have an almighty god whom worshipers can interact with through the help of intermediaries (saints or the Yoruba's orishas). So, the Yoruba people adapted and prevailed.

It took a lot of time for the Yoruba people to see themselves as a single nation. Even now, the subgroups are different enough to consider themselves separate, adapting the religion to their own history and society. That is the beauty of the Yoruba religion, its flexibility allows its followers to adapt it to their culture and heritage.

Yoruba Beliefs

The Yoruba religion has its own doctrines, concepts, spiritual beings, and symbols. Let's take a look at some basic notions that define the Yoruba religion.

- *Ayanmo* - fate or destiny

The Yoruba people believe that we all experience *Ayanmo*

throughout our lives. The Yoruba believe that we choose our own destiny before birth, but that we forget all about it when we arrive on Earth. So, one of our life purposes should be claiming our *Ayanmo*.

- **Olodumare** - the state of becoming one with the source of all energy/divine creator.

The Yoruba believe that it is the duty of all people to become enlightened in a spiritual aspect. To become enlightened, one must grow his *Ori-inu* (spiritual consciousness) and unite it with his *Ori-orun* (spirit). The people that try to find their destiny and achieve transcendence go to *Orun-Rere* (the realm of those that do good). Those that don't tend to their spirituality are destined for *Orun-Apadi* (the invisible realm of potsherds).

Olodumare also refers to the god of the Yoruba people, commonly known as the "one who has the fullness of everything." This supreme god is not defined by any gender (referred to as "they"), and the Yoruba believe that Olodumare has all the attributes of a person (thus, this god is not a perfect being like the Orthodox or Catholic "God"). Olodumare is considered the creator of all things, but other than that, this divine being is quite distant. The god does not meddle in the affairs of humans, and the Yoruba people don't pray directly to Olodumare. Yoruba worshipers communicate to Olodumare through *orishas*.

- **Ayé** - the physical realm, the life.

The Yoruba believe that a person's thoughts and actions in *Ayé* interact with all the living things that exist, including the Earth itself. During *Ayé*, one must grow his *Ori-inu* through sincere meditation and prayer.

3

- **Ashe** - a force possessed by both humans and gods.

Ashe is a powerful life force that is very similar in concept to the Chakras in Indian beliefs or the Chinese notion of Chi. This force has the potential to bring about change, whether good or bad. The Yoruba believe that everything in nature contains *Ashe*, from natural phenomena (lightning, thunder, rain) to bodily fluids (blood) and even names (mostly names that are considered to be sacred). So, when Yoruba followers worship a river or a tree, they don't see it as an idol/god, but as a container of *Ashe*, a force worthy of admiration and respect.

- **Orishas** - the negotiators between the world of the humans and the supreme deity.

Orishas are similar in role to the Catholic saints, but they are very human in nature. They are not an embodiment of perfection, but rather one of good and bad characteristics. They can make mistakes and misbehave. *Orishas* live on Earth as divine spirits, humans that ascended to divinities, or as natural elements (mountains, rivers, trees). Yoruba people also associate mundane things like numbers or pieces of clothing with specific *orishas*, leaving way for a whole realm of codes and messages ready to be interpreted. There are over 3,000 *orishas*, all of which are said to be just incarnations of the divine being Olodumare.

We'll go back to learning more about *orishas* in a separate chapter.

- **Ajogun** - beings that represent negative forces.

*Ajogun*s are very similar to demons, as they can cause calamities, misfortunes (accidents), or illnesses (depression).

The Yoruba people are known for not separating religious matters from worldly problems. If something bad happens to someone, the general consensus would be that they had an encounter with an *Ajogun* or that they upset an *orisha*. Those that believe they are cursed or possessed by an *Ajogun* need to visit an Ifa priest who can perform a divination ritual that gets rid of the malevolent spirit.

- **Reincarnation** - the continuous cycle of existence in different forms/rebirth

Reincarnation is not a concept that belongs solely to the Yoruba religion, but the major difference from other believers in the rebirth of the soul is that the Yoruba people see it as something positive. This is in contrast to other beliefs, such as Buddhism, where reincarnation is a form of torment that needs to be escaped.

The Yoruba Creation Story

All religions have a creation myth that sets the basis of its view on the world. It's absolutely fascinating how many versions humanity has for the beginning of life as we know it. Let's waste no more time and explore the creation myth of the Yoruba people, which focuses on the origins of humanity as well as the origin of the sacred city Ife.

The Orishas in the Sky

A long time ago, when the Universe was formed, there was just the sky, the waters, and marshy lands in between. Olorun (a different name for *Olodumare*, used when they are referred to as "ruler of the sky and creator of the sun") lived in the sky with the orishas, while the goddess Olokun ruled the watery lands.

Olorun was not bound by gender identities, but the orishas that accompanied the ruler of the sky were male and female. Olorun encouraged the orishas to explore the vast sky, but they preferred to remain close to a young baobab tree that

5

provided them with everything they needed. They had gold jewelry, beautiful garments, and all that their hearts desired, so why venture into the unknown?

Interpretations

There are a few conclusions and parallels we can make regarding the Yoruba creation myth and its variations.

For one, we have a consistent reminder that orishas are not perfect. Obatala falls victim to alcohol and ends up creating deformed beings; Olokun is spiteful, and in her rage, she annihilates innocent people, and let's not forget the other orishas who were content with living near the baobab tree instead of wanting to do more with their powers. Orishas also have feelings and experience human emotions: Obatala feels lonely by himself and ashamed of his mistakes, while Olokun is angry and vengeful.

Then we have the confirmation that humans are "deformed" beings who should not seek perfection, thus putting spiritual evolution above the physical aspect.

We also have parallels to other mythologies through the myth of the Great Flood, here brought by Olokun's wrath. This motif of the flood is found in many cultures. Some examples are the flood in Genesis, Guan-Yu's flood of Chinese mythology, the Pralaya of Hindu mythology, and other myths from Greek mythology, Mesopotamian stories, Norse mythology, and so on.

TWO

Elegua

THE MESSENGER

Considered the first Orisha created, Elegua opens and closes the way to humanity. He manages the crossroads that men journey across. It is said that all prayers go through Elegua first before getting to any other Orisha. You would pray to Elegua in the affairs of destiny and fate.

Elegba is often represented as either an old man or a child. He also represents birth and death and the opening and closing of pathways through life. He is a trickster and has been described as complex. Elegba is said to serve the chief god, Ifa, and is a messenger between Earth and heaven.

For those who choose to live a moral and religious lifestyle, he can be both a strong supporter and contributor. For those who go against his ideals, he acts as an enforcer. The Yoruba people are also quick to mention that he can raise you high upon his hands, and in a flash, he will drop you and allow you to fall.

Elegua rules the crossroads, doorways, and gates of this world. He is the safe keeper of Ashe and unlocks the path and allows desire to run in the universe. The color patterns of red and black, in addition to black and white, are his sacred bead configuration. They mirror his opposing natures. Representing the cross paths of our lives where we have to make an important decision. Elegba represents not only the uncertainty of taking the right route but is also the Orisha that is concerned with the consequences of your choices and serves as a guide, helping those find the right path.

Elegba takes a fancy to all things childlike, such as whistles, bells, kites, and balls. Children are emissaries between the two worlds. He brings them good fortune.

Also, not unexpectedly, Elegua has a close connection with Orunmila, the Orisha of divination. Without the consent of Elegua, no spell or ritual can be performed in either realm. It is to Elegua to whom you make compensating sacrifices. It is Elegua that you would call before any other Orisha to open the doors and begin the magical rituals. Without his acceptance, access to the other Orishas will not be granted. His numbers are three and twenty-one.

With a personality of interested, curious, and talkative, he is invoked to remove obstacles, help communicating other spirits and Loas, open and close doors and portals, for matters of opportunities and connections with the ones that are far away. He is said to be fluent in any tongue that we speak gracefully, ever spoke, or ever will be spoken.

Elegua is an essential Orisha in Santeria. Elegua is associated with Saint Anthony, Saint Martin, and the Infant of Prague.

Elegua Symbols and Associations

Also known as Elegba, Legba, Papa Legba, Esu, Eshu, or Elegbara, Elegua's number is seven. Represented by a beaded necklace of red and black, one of his colors represents life, whereas the other represents death. Other symbols include a mound of red clay, cards, dice, three stones, and keys.

Elegua is also associated with beings of comparable strength such as the Native American Coyote, the Roman God Mercury, the Hopi's Kokopelli, and the Norse God Odin.

Enjoying his feast day on January 6th and June 13th,

Except for pigeon, Elegua will eat just about anything for offerings. Elegua enjoys smoked fish, goat, rooster, bush rat, rum, chili peppers, and tobacco. Offerings of wrapped candies and toys for the fledgling, beginning roads are perfect, while the mature roads may appreciate hard candies, popcorn, or toasted corn. His day of the week is Monday.

Animals that are favored by Elegua are the snake, coyote, raven, or any other trickster animal. Elegua resides in a shallow dish made from clay, which is placed behind the door within a household. Though the children of Elegba possess no known traits, he protects against bad decisions. On the flip side, he can also place obstacles on your path.

THREE

Yemaya

THE ABSOLUTE MOTHER

The Orisha of motherhood and the queen of the sea is Yemaya. She is called upon to in difficulties of fruitfulness and mystic growth. Yemaya is a foundation of well-being and strength in times of emotional crisis.

Yemaya is described as the great mother and ruler of the ocean. Life on Earth wouldn't be possible if it were not for water. Hence Yemaya is seen as an essential part of creation. Legend says that when her waters broke, it flooded the Earth, giving rise to the oceans, rivers, and lakes. The first mortal human beings are also said to have been created in her womb.

Since all life began in the sea, the amniotic fluid inside the womb represents the sea. The embryo needs to change and grow in the configuration of a fish ahead of becoming a human baby. To the human eyes, Yemaya appears as a mermaid, which is how she usually is represented. This brings up her observed form of Mami Wata religion of the ancient water deities portrayed with upper bodies as human and fish or snake lower bodies, which are not part of the Yoruba pantheon of the Orishas. Yemaya is connected with Our Lady of Regla.

She is considered both motherly and brutal. When she is

angered, she can lash out with ferocity, but if the person shows sincere remorse for their actions, she can be forgiving if warranted.

Yemaya is known to love anything related to the water, such as seahorses, anchors, fishing nets, fish, and seashells. Yemaya also has a soft spot for verbena perfume. She is the ruler of the regions of the sea that people on Earth know, such as the plant and sea life that is used for food. Another Orisha, Olokun, governs the darkest parts of the waters. She is frequently represented as a mermaid and worshiped alongside all water bodies, including wells, streams, and creeks.

Along with the basis of all manifestations, Olokun, the center of all wealth, Yemaya provides as quickly as her sister Oshun does. Seven is her number. The colors pattern of interchanging seven white and seven blue is her sacred bead configuration. Yemaya wears seven skirts in the colors of blue and white.

Similar to the seas and lakes, she is profound and unknowable in entirety. As Okuti, she is the queen of witches, who carries deep, dark secrets, especially for hexes and curses. With a temperament of being nurturing, loving, direct, and frank, she is invoked to remove the obstacles, protect the female, in all things to do with motherhood, meditation, clairvoyance, calm seas, and alike.

Yemaya is a master at divination (the practice of seeking answers using supernatural powers). Women were initially being banned from practicing this form of magic. She regularly spied on her husband, Orula, when he was consulting. Orula noticed how good she was at divination and made a pact with her, allowing her to practice using cowrie shells.

Yemaya is the eldest sister of Oshun and mother and foster mother to a majority of the other Orishas. Because of her significance as a mother figure, she provides a haven and mother-like person for those seeking refuge when they are lonely or lost. She is always there with open arms offering love and guidance to anyone who needs a mom.

Yemaya Symbols and Associations

Known as Yemeya, La Sirene, Mommi, Nana Buruku, Mother of Water, and so much more, Yemaya enjoys rich and delicious foods, such as guinea hens, rooster, and ram, which she shares with Chango as well as kola nuts, red palm oil, fish, cantaloupe, berries, watermelon, and coconut.

Feast days for Yemaya are January 1st, February 2nd in Brazil, Mother's Day, September 7th in Santeria, with her day of the week being Saturday.

With colors of blue and white, Yemaya is said to live in a blue flowered soup tureen filled with water, with seven silver bracelets (seven is her number), mirrors, and a necklace made with beads. She loves peacocks, ducks, stars, full-moon, and anything that comes from the sea.

Yemaya is the patron of pregnant women and protects babies while still in the womb. Children of Yemaya are said to be women who value their independence and who are strong-willed. They are easy-going and are not quick to get angry or lose their temper. They may seem arrogant at times but place great importance in being a mother or part of their community. This is probably why The Heart chakra represents her the best. This chakra is emotional and drives forward to enhance our emotional development.

Beings of Equivalent Strength are the Egyptian Goddess Isis, the Norse Goddess Frigg, and the Chinese Goddess Kuan Yin.

FOUR

Oshun

GODDESS OF LOVE AND HAPPINESS

As the goddess of love and abundance, Oshun is often seen as the Venus or Aphrodite of the Orishas, Oshun is summoned for assistance in love and longing. She aids those who are going through a stage of change and growth.

Oshun is another powerful, female Orisha. She is the youngest and most beautiful of all Orishas and is recognized as the queen of the rivers. Oshun is also regarded as the Orisha of femininity, sensual power, and love.

When the Earth's creation was complete, Olodumare contemplated what else was needed and noticed that the most significant things that were missing were characteristics such as love and sweetness, two things that would inspire those to continue to live their lives. Oshun was thus created and sent down to the world to cultivate these traits and values in others.

It was initially said that all the water on Earth belongs to Yemaya, Oshun's mother (or sister in some belief). The story goes that one day Oshun was mercilessly pursued by Ogun when she slipped and fell into a river. The currents and whirlpools dragged her away. Yemaya protected Oshun and gifted her rivers so that she would have her own kingdom to rule.

When issues arise around marriage, love, motherhood, and relationships, both women work together to ensure that it flourishes. Oshun is there to make sure that life is created and that babies are conceived. She also represents fertility but leaves the aspects of looking after children to Yemaya.

She is known to be lively and vivacious, representative of a river. Oshun is the essence of a woman and loves mirrors, fans, and jewelry (made from brass, amber, gold, and coral). She has a taste for honey and sunflowers too.

Stories of Oshun by the Yoruba people also mention that she is not only the goddess who creates life but that she can also take it from you. If ever disrespected, Oshun is said to be able to cause drought by withholding her waters or flood the earth.

Oshun says she belonged to no man and thought all was fair in the game of love. You can create an altar for her with a yellow candle, cinnamon, anise, pumpkins amber, coral, and cowries, and some honey that you should taste first since Oshun was poisoned by honey.

Each year, devotees make the annual pilgrimage to the Oshun River in Nigeria to pay their respects and ask for health, wealth, and children. Osogobo is the capital city of Osun in Nigeria, and it is here that you will find the Osun-Osogbo Sacred Grove, woodland that is home to artwork and shrines in honor of her. In 2005, it was declared a World Heritage Site by UNESCO.

Oshun Symbols and Associations

Also known as Ochun, Oxum, Osun is characterized by the color scheme of yellow and gold. Her beaded necklaces vary, but they commonly include yellow, amber, green, honey-colored beads, and coral. Her attire is yellow or amber-colored with gold trim. Her number is five and multiples thereof. Peacocks, yellow butterflies, bees, otters, skunks, and vultures belong to her and are generally used to exemplify her. Take pleasure in her feast day of September 8th with pumpkins, honey, coconut, spinach, almonds, yams, cinnamon, lemons, chicken, and Goldschlager Liquor being favorite offerings for Oshun. As well as her day of the week is Saturday.

Gemstones corresponding with Oshun are generally amber, citrine, diamonds, imperial topaz, rutilated quartz, golden beryl, and yellow fluorite.

As with Page of Cups, Ace, and Two of Cups, Oshun addresses, she is also signifying truth, patience, care, and perseverance. Being linked with the Heart Chakra influence our ability to give and receive love—from others and ourselves. The Solar Plexus speaks to your ability to be confident and in control of your life. is appropriate for Oshun. Not only is it the first chakra, but its energy is also based on the Earth element, the sense of security and grounding.

Residing in a yellow soup tureen made from porcelain and filled with water, Oshun protects against fertility issues. Looking after the reproductive health of women, Oshun also protects against diseases that afflict the lower intestines and stomach and is associated with Our Lady of Charity. This explains why Oshun's children are spirited and happy. They are determined and have a penchant for beautiful things. Her children value the opinions of others and enjoy the smaller things in life.

Individuals of Equal Strength to Oshun is the Greek goddess Aphrodite, the Babylonian goddess Ishtar, the Roman goddess Venus, Norse goddess Freya, and any other Goddesses of Love.

FIVE

Chango

GOD OF JUSTICE

A War god, connected with Mars, claimed to give victory over adversaries and perform powerful punishment upon them. He is called mostly for men in all issues to do with success and sensuality, to be seductive to women.

The Orisha of lightning, power, sensuality, and passion is Chango. Together with Oshun, Obatala, and Yemaya, Chango is one of the four influences of Santeria. He is extensively cherished and inspired by power and pride.

Chango is the lord of lightning and fire, thunder, and war. Chango is also the deity who presides over music, drumming, and dancing. He is an Orisha who represents the power and stamina of man. He also represents passion and beauty.

Chango may perhaps be the best recognized of the Orishas. He rules dance, drums, fire, lightning, and thunder. As an Orisha warrior of knowledge and intellect, Chango has hot-tempered nature and is the personification of manhood. Chango took the appearance of Oyo, the Supreme King.

Chango is dressed in red satin pants and a shirt with white trim and wears a crown. He was once a king who ruled the Yoruba ancestral homeland, Oyo. He is often described as boasting king-like qualities such as being a leader, hard worker, and formidable warrior.

Apart from his leadership characteristics, he is also said to be a womanizer and master manipulator. It is said that the list of lovers he had was endless. He is kind towards his children but is quick to remind them of their failures if they are unable to live up to his standards.

He is well-versed in divination and is also known to be a remarkable healer. He has a penchant for cornmeal dumplings, okra, and bananas.

Certain tales tell of him stealing Oya away from his brother Ogun, and that is why there is such a rivalry between the two deities. When the time comes for war, Chango is said to choose Oya, a fellow fighter, because she is as fearless as he is. Worshippers often describe the presence of thunder and lightning as the two Orishas riding into battle together.

Followers summon Chango by shaking maracas while at his altar. Those who are said to have Chango on their head salute this Orisha by lying face down on the ground with their arms extended alongside them. Devotees also play the bata drum to summon storms, as Chango did during his reign as king.

Chango Symbols and Associations

Also known as Shango, Siete Rayos, Sango, Jakuta, or Xango, Chango offerings consist of apples, cornbread, okra, and tobacco, hot/spicy foods such as chili peppers and tamales as well as red wine dry. When mentioning his name, individuals that are followers of Chango stand on tiptoe or a rise in their seats to display respect. With his numbers being four and six, he enjoys a necklace made of alternating red and white beads, red and white stripes. Chango frequently wields a double ax. He is associated with St. Barbara.

As a representative of swift justice, Chango's symbols are thunderstorms, lightning bolts, double-headed ax, drum double-headed ax. Protecting against death arising from fire and burns, it's no wonder his astrological sign is Leo and planet is Mars.

December 4th is Chango's feast day having his day of the week being Friday. Chango resides in a small wooden bowl with a lid that is placed on a tall pedestal.

Children of Chango: Children of Oshun are said to bear the same traits as him. They can have fiery temperaments but love to party, flirt, and have a good time. They can be described as hotheaded and self-absorbed. They are also said to be highly intelligent and enjoy being the center of attention.

Spirits of equal power to Chango are the Norse God Thor, the Roman God Mars, the Greek God Ares, and other War Gods.

SIX

Obatala

GOD OF CREATIVITY AND HARMONY

As the oldest of the Orishas, Obatala is respected as the initiator of all humanity. Obatala is called upon in times of legal trouble. Identified to be a fair and candid judge, Obatala offers strength to the blameless and justice to the guilty.

He is the caring father of not only all the Orishas but that of humanity. Obatala is also the holder of the head and intellects. He rules the minds, bringing the mind, peace, and remedies life-threatening illnesses. As a very sympathetic Loa, Obatala was the maker of the Earth and humanity

Before land existed, his father, Olodumare (the supreme God), sent him down to Earth, which was then only covered by water. His father's instructions were to create the Earth, and he bestowed Obatala with a handful of dirt and one chicken to do so.

Obatala placed the dirt in the center of the ocean and put the chicken on top of it. The chicken began scratching the soil, spreading far and wide, and this is how the Earth was shaped. After land was created, Olofi (a manifestation of the supreme God), instructed Obatala to create human beings. His final touch was to add heads to the bodies of the humans he shaped; thus, he is also known as the owner of all heads.

He is the owner of all things white. Human heads, their dreams, and thoughts. He governs silver and white metal. Obatala is also the owner of the ceiba tree. It has been said that he loves snails, cocoa butter, cotton, and marble eggs too. With the tarot cards, the Emperor and Justice Obatala was sent to the planet to do good and serve as king of the Earth.

Obatala Symbols and Associations

Known also as Obatalá, Ochala, Oxalá, Orichalá, Orixalá, and more, Obatala resides in a white porcelain soup tureen stored on the altar within the home. He is associated with Madonna of Mercy, Our Lady of Mercy.

Some say his day of the week is Thursday, while others say Sunday. Obatala's feast day is September 24th, with offerings, consist of black-eyed peas, the milk or the meat of a coconut, eggs, rice, mushrooms, potatoes, milk, water, cotton, snail shells, crushed up eggshells, frankincense, sandalwood, or myrrh incense, and tobacco.

With his number being eight, Obatala's symbols are generally mountains, quartz crystals, frogs, white animals, white rocks, mountains, snail shells, and cowrie shells. With the Sun and Jupiter

Obatala protects against dementia, blindness, and paralysis. The children of Obatala are trustworthy individuals who are calm and confident. They are not quick to complain and may appear reserved at times.

With the power of the Sun, Obatala works with Active change, advancement, promotion, self-confidence, success, and vitality along with Jupiter bestowing abundance, business, and fame

Spiritual beings of equivalent strength to Obatala are the African God Damballah, Norse God Tyr, Norse God Odin, and the Egyptian God Ra.

SEVEN

Ogun

GOD OF WAR

Having the status of the protective father figure, Ogun is the Orisha of tools and weapons. As an enthusiast of the wilderness, Ogun gives strength and protection to individuals with a conflict to battle.

Ogun governs all minerals and metals, iron in particular. He is commonly associated with weapons, tools, knives, and mountains. Images of him portray a man, bare-chested, dressed in a palm skirt that is said to protect him from evil. He is often depicted as a lone blacksmith who lives in solitude deep in the forest.

Sacred stories (Patakis) mention that Obatala is his father and that his mother is Yemu. He has two brothers, Ochosi and Elegua. Ogun was said to be one of the first Orishas to visit Earth to seek an adequate place for humans to live. In other beliefs, he was said to have cleared a pathway using an ax and provided the companionship of a dog to allow for other Orishas to enter the earth.

Tales mention that Ogun desired to have a relationship with his mother. One day Elegua, ever watchful that this did not happen, missed sight of Ogun. Ogun forced himself upon his mother and was caught in the act by Obatala. Before

Obatala could punish him, Ogun cursed himself, leaving to go live in the forest, alone and without the company of anyone else. He committed to working his entire life away. His misery led to magical powers of tragedy to be leaked into the world.

Oshun, the goddess of love, seduced him in a bid to save humanity, and after his time spent with her, Ogun began to enjoy his life once more, and the bitterness he cast into the world abated.

He is known to love alcohol, cigars, soaked fish, and roasted sweet potatoes. It is not an uncommon sight to find these placed near railroad tracks as an offering to him. Followers can swear an oath to tell the truth in court by kissing a piece of iron.

A mystifying Loa summoned for issues of protection, employment, prophecy, magickal work and teaching, blood magick, blood illnesses, and situations cure. He is the overseer of all technology, as well as influences how the technology will work together with its natural world. The use of technology and science in warfare is the sphere of Ogun along with black-smithing, farming, civilization in general, and transportation. Once Elegua opens the doors and roads, Ogun then cleanses them with his machete.

Ogun oversees all those who work with metal, such as surgeons, police officers, mechanics, and engineers. He is also a talented farmer and a skilled hunter. Along with his brother, Elegua, they protect the entryways of homes.

Ogun Symbols and Associations

Known also as Oggun, Ogou, Ogúm, or Ògún, Ogun's number is seven and with a color scheme is red and white in Voodoo, while green and black in Santeria including three and seven. Ogun is also correlated with St. Peter as well as beings of comparable strength: Norse Wayland the Smith, Roman god Vulcan, Greek god Hephaestus.

Enjoying his feast day of June 29th, Ogun's food offerings are typically meat, nuts, chili, peppers, hot and spicy foods, roots, and soda crackers with palm oil, rum, and whiskey. His days of the week are Tuesday and Wednesday, and the 4th of every month.

Symbols are generally a bracelet or anklet that carries charms shaped in weapons, tools, locks, and keys.

Ogun resides in a cauldron. This is placed alongside Oshun, Ochosi, and Elegua. Together the four of them are known as the warriors.

Protecting against complications and death during surgery, accidents, and injuries caused by metal objects, drivers are known to hold onto a pendant of Ogun to avoid getting into car accidents.

With a fierce understanding of civil justice, a profound moral compass guides Ogun's decisions. As the astrology sign of Aries, Ogun may be impulsive but never mean. Not surprised, there is a relation to Saturn. Saturn is generally associated with fathers or father/authority figures. In childhood, the rules, discipline, and principles introduced by authority figures such as parents, teachers, and the like, were not always pleasant. Still, they helped us to understand the world around us. Similarly, Ogun's lessons help us to grow.

Ogun's children may be either violent or unforgiving. They are also described as being determined and brave. They are hard workers who are known for their honesty.

As with the King of Pentacles, Ogun addresses authority, tradition, and success in money matters. He is also signifying truth, patience, care, and perseverance. Being linked with the Root chakra is appropriate for Ogun. Not only is it the first chakra, but its energy is also based on the Earth element, the sense of security and grounding.

You will find the solitary hunters such as Tigers, Panthers, Hawks, Bears, and Rattlesnakes are the best animals to represent him.

EIGHT

Oya

GODDESS OF TORNADO

The Orisha of the connection between the living and the dead is Oya. A favored lover of Chango, Oya can control lightning, hail, tornadoes to fight her adversaries.

Oya is an Orisha who owns both storms and wind. She represents change and brings upon transition even if a human being did not ask for it. She brings change, storms, tornadoes, wind, lightning, death, witchcraft, athletics, and business. Oya is the most aggressive of all the female Orishas. She is known as a fierce warrior and staunch protector of women who appeal to her to resolve disputes in their favor. Oya often fights in wars alongside Chango, using lightning and two swords as weapons.

She can create winds ranging from the calm breeze to the strong hurricane. She goes onwards with her husband through his thunderstorms, tearing up trees, wrecking buildings, and blowing things down. Oya is recognized as a mighty and fierce warrior. A staunch protector of women who appeal to her to resolve disputes in their favor.

Chango chooses her to fight by his side because of her role in rescuing him from other Orishas. The story goes that Chango had a love for seducing other Orishas' wives. One night at a party, the other Orishas captured Chango and locked him up in a prison cell, tossing the key away. Oya wondered where Chango was and had a vision of him being imprisoned. She sent forward lightning bolts that broke the jail cell bars and rushed in upon a storm to save him. She is a mighty warrior whose army consists of the spirits of the dead (Egun).

Oya is known to guard the gates of cemeteries, ensuring that both the boundaries of death and life are honored. She is a private Orisha who obscures her face by wearing a mask. She wears a long, colorful skirt, and when she dances, it is said to bring about tornadoes. Rainbows are said to belong to her and represent the colors found in her colorful skirt.

She loves grapes, white rice, and eggplant. Devotees shake the seed pod of a framboyan tree to summon her. The sounds emitted from the pod are said to echo the sound of thunder. It is not unusual to come across small offerings placed in busy marketplaces in honor of her. Oya resides over markets because they symbolize change.

Oya brings about purification. The wind is also representative of Oyo's ways, blowing away the bad things in life that no longer serve us and blowing new stuff onto our path that will help us to grow.

Oya is the elder sister to the goddesses Oshun and Yemaya. She is believed to be the Crone characteristic of this Triple goddess trio. As a Crone Goddess, she is a teacher of reality and a source of justice. During the wind, rain, snow, and thunderstorms, take in Oya's power by meditating. Think of Storm from the X-men.

With nine being her favorite number, she has nine children. The children of Oya are strong. They are generally relaxed people but are said to become aggressive when things do not go as planned or end up in their favor. They are incredibly loyal but get bored quickly.

Oya Symbolism and Associations

Also known as Yansa, Iansa, Yansan Lansá, or Oiá, symbols for Oya are the Iruke, a whip made from a horse's tail, to symbolize the wind, a copper sword, the water buffalo, and lightning. Oya protects us from stagnant behavior, people, and things.

Oya resides in a soup tureen made from porcelain and painted in nine different colors or shades of burgundy and brown. Friday is her day of the week with February 2th as the day of Oya's feast.

The children of Oya are powerful. They are generally relaxed people but are said to become aggressive when things do not go as planned or end up in their favor. They are incredibly loyal but get bored quickly.

All strong Warrior Goddesses such as Greek Goddess Athena, Hindu Goddess Kali, and Hawaiian Goddess Pele, are beings of equivalent strength to Oya.

NINE

Spells

Spells are for the most part worked in the Yoruba practice. They differ for distinctive reasons. For instance, love matters and success; it is to open your roads for blessings and to fend off any evil that might be coming in your direction. Ebbos or cleansings are performed to clean the route so everything can fall into place and help you with what is needed. They could be a sacrifice to the Orishas or a straightforward cleansing with fruits or a bath. Adimus or offerings are created for the Orishas to satisfy them for something they assisted you with. This might be their favorite food, a bottle of perfume, or even a simple array of flowers.

I have included in this section prayers, spells and food for your Orisha and you.

Prayer to the Seven African Powers

Seven African Powers, who remain so near to our divine;
Protector, with great modesty,
I kneel before you and plead,
Your intervention in front of the Great Spirit.

Listen to my request and give me abundance and harmony.

Please take away all of the barriers

That drives me to wander away from the Splendor

Olofi, I have belief in your words

Request and you shall attain

Let it be so!

Amen.

*Make your request

Prayer to the Orisha

May my descendants continue to lead and protect me

May Elegua open the doors of opportunities and remove obstacles from my path

May Ogun provide me courage to overcome my problems and defeat my enemies

May Oshosi bring Justice and Balance to my life

May Orunmila bestow his wisdom upon me

May Obatala bring peace, tranquility, and harmony to my life

May Babalu heal my body and soul

May Olokun give strength to my being

May Yemaya renew and refresh my life with the powers of her waters

May Chango give me the strength to fight and win my battles

May Oshun fulfill my dreams of love and riches

May Oya bring with her the winds of change and prosperity to my space.

Seven African Powers Incense

Items Needed:

4 tablespoons Powdered Frankincense

3 tablespoons Powdered Myrrh
2 tablespoons Powdered Cinnamon
1 tablespoon Powdered Sandalwood
1 tablespoon Powdered Sage
1/2 tablespoon Powdered Dragon's Blood
Directions:
Combine all of the ingredients together. Put the mixture into a dark amber or blue glass storage jar pending usage. To use, burn a small amount on a hot charcoal disc.

Seven African Powers Blessing
Items Needed:
Seven Day Candle
Seven African Powers Incense
2 White Altar Candles
Plain White Cloth
Directions:
Begin by constructing an altar with the plain white cloth and two white altar candles. Many individuals may prefer the white altar cloth adorned with a bit lace. In the center of the altar candles, arrange your Seven Day Candle and burn your Seven African Powers incense.

Recite the following:
I call upon Elegua to remove all obstacles,
Chango for power over my enemies,
Obatala to create peace,
Ogun to provide work,
Orula to open doors,
Oshun to bring love
Yemaya to make me fruitful.

Light your seven-day candle at the same time each evening, stating your request.

At one time, it was customary to leave seven-day candles burning around-the-clock. Since this procedure can cause a fire hazard, I tell people for safety reasons to as an alternative extinguish their candle after finishing the request and some prayers, and then relight the next evening.

Peace in the Home with Obatala

Items Needed:

White Eggshell Powder

Directions:

For peace in your home, sprinkle white eggshell powder all around your house and light a white candle to Obatala.

Oshun Makeup Spell

Items Needed:

Cinnamon Powder

Loose Makeup Powder

Directions:

Take your loose makeup powder and add a little cinnamon powder to it. Apply your make up as you usually do. While looking in a mirror communicate with Oshun expressing to her that every person who looks at you will fall for your sweet smelling fragrance.

Oya Potpourri

Items Needed:

9 Purple Heart Plant Flowers

½ cut Lichen

½ cup Sweet Grass

½ cup dried Cyclamen Flowers with Leaves

1 Vanilla Bean Cut into 3 Pieces

1 tablespoon Dried Blue Lotus

Directions:

Add to some water in your cauldron over a flame or a potpourri burner.

*Note: You can substitute vanilla bean with 3 cinnamon sticks.

Spell to Attract Customers
Items Needed:
White Sugar
Brown Sugar
3 Cinnamon Sticks
3 Coins
Money Powder
Saint Michael Revocation Pull Out Candle
Fast Money Oil
Aloe Vera Plant
Plant Pot or Vase
Holy Water
Soil
Directions:

In a pot or vase put a mixture of white and brown sugar to the half of your vase or pot. Place three cinnamon sticks, three Coins, and an aloe vera plant. Fill with soil and money powder. After planting the aloe vera, you should pray:

Chango, please bless this plant for my business success day by day, release me from the ruins and betrayals, always away from all troubles and pains that try to reach my business.

At the close, complete with an Our Father and light a Saint Michael Revocation Pull Out Candle to attract customers with a few drops of Fast Money Oil. Perform this every Friday watering the soil with holy water. As the plant grows and you look after it, your business will grow and prosper.

. . .

Spell for Salary Increase

Items Needed:

Green Cloth

White Plate

7 Coins

Holy Water

Green 7 Day Glass Candle Road Opener

Fast Money Oil

Road Opener Oil

Sandalwood Incense

Directions:

Wash the seven coins with holy water. Place a plate with the seven coins on top of a green cloth. Place in the center of the plate a green 7 Day Glass Candle Road Opener in addition to some Fast Money Oil and Road Opener Oil as an offering to Elegua to open the roads in their service for the increase you need. Switch on for seven days with sandalwood incense to purify and for good luck.

Offering to Oya

Items Needed:

9 Eggplants

Corojo Butter or Palm Oil

Directions:

Coat the nine eggplants with the Corojo butter or palm oil and place them on a white plate. Set them in front of an image of Oya asking her for what you want.

To Attract Good Luck with Chango

Items Needed:

A Piece of Obsidian, Onyx, or Chalcedony

Red Wine

Magnet

Gold and Silver Magnetic Sand
Candle
Directions:
Wash the stone with red wine and put the stone inside of
the glass with the magnet. Sprinkle some gold and silver
magnetic sand on the top of your stone and light your candle
to Chango.

Mirror Box
Items Needed:
1 box
Small Mirrors (shape and quantity depends on the
intention)
Glue
Directions:
In modern Voodoo, a mirror box has a selection of bene-
fits. Essentially, it is a box that is mirrored on the inside. The
objectives of this will hinge on why they are there.

Mirrors, aside from being sacred to Oshun, and to a
number of points Boyuto, who is the Orisha of Illusion,
capture and reflect a person's image. It can furthermore guard
or strengthen, as the mirror itself has its own divine grace,
knowledge, authority, wisdom, and natural characteristics. A
great deal like crystals, they can be given an intention
depending on their natural preferences.

Inside a box, it can safeguard the outside world from the
box's contents by reflecting the energy of the item inside back
to itself. It can catch an individual's image at the same time as
making a request or prayer in order to program items such as
crystals. It can help in stamping a talisman that is kept in a
box upon its keeper. It can as well help to strengthen the
power of an object.

The mirrors in a mirror box are numbered and organized,
corresponding to their reason for being there. Their shape is

also significant. Round mirrors are normally used for radiating energy, love and emotional issues. Diamond or square shaped mirrors are usually used for protection, suppression, and occasionally hexing when a curse is for justice or stopping someone from doing destructive things. Triangular mirrors or those set in a triangular pattern are frequently used for power, fertility, and personality. Different individuals may have numerous ways of doing things, but these are usually the norm.

Oshun Bath
Items Needed:
½ teaspoon Cinnamon
½ teaspoon Nutmeg
1 ounce Florida Water
1 ounce Rose Water
1 ounce River Water
4-ounce Bottle
Directions:
Combine all ingredients together in a bottle and mix well. Add to your bath intended to honor Oshun.

Oshun Oil
Items Needed:
30 drops Magnolia Essential Oil
18 drops Rose Geranium Essential Oil or Rose Essential Oil
15 drops Cinnamon Essential Oil
12 drops Sweet Orange Essential Oil
1 oz. Grapeseed Oil
Dried Rose Petals
Dried Patchouli
Dried Orange Leaves or Rinds
Directions:

Add one drop at a time. Blend in a base of grapeseed oil. Use Oshun Oil to honor the river goddess and draw love and prosperity to you. To improve prosperity, add dried orange leaves or rinds; to increase love, add rose petals and patchouli leaves to enrich passion.

Chango Love Spell

Items Needed:

6 Red Apples

Palm Oil

Honey

Cinnamon Powder

1 Red 7 Day Candle

Small Table

Red Tablecloth

White Plate

Directions:

Create a clean area in your home for your spell using a table with a red tablecloth where you will place Chango's image or statue. Write the individual's name six times on a paper bag and write your name directly on top of it covering their name. Spread some honey over both names and place it on a white plate. Take the seven-day red candle and smear some honey with the cinnamon powder all over the candle. Light it, take the six apples, rub palm oil all over the apples one by one, and place them on the plate around the candle. After all of the apples are on the plate, pour the honey on top of all the apples in a circular rotation and then sprinkle the cinnamon powder on top of everything asking Chango to spark the passion between the people that are on the plate. Let it remain there for six days and after that take the plate and everything on it, to a palm tree that is near a river. On the other hand, a bushy wood area and leave it near a tall tree.

· · ·

Obatala's Calming an Individual
Items Needed:
White Eggshell Powder
Cocoa Butter
Soothing Balsam Oil
White Candle
Long White Ribbon
White Cloth
Pen or Pencil
Jar with Lid
Directions:
Set Obatala or a representation of him somewhere it will not be interrupted. You must measure out the ribbon approximately the height of the individual. With the ribbon, make eight knots from one end to the other while asking Obatala with every knot to calm the individual. You want to bless this person, clear their path and so on. Write the person's name with the pen or pencil after each knot. Place your knotted ribbon in the jar with the soothing balsam oil, and cover it with cocoa butter and white eggshell powder. Light the white candle to Obatala and leave the jar covered with your white cloth until the work is accomplished.

Elegua Incense
Items Needed:
1/4 cup Myrrh or Benzoin
1/2 cup Aloes Wood or Sandalwood
1/4 cup powder Coffee
1-teaspoon Cardamom
1/8 cup powder Star Anise
1/8 cup Cinnamon Powder
1-teaspoon Clove Powder
1/4 teaspoon Red Pepper Powder
1/4 teaspoon Ground Black Pepper

Mortar and Pestle or Heavy-Duty Food Grinder
Elegua Oil
Directions:
On a Monday, collect all of your ingredients and position them on a plate, and pass them within the smoke of incense, asking Eshu to consecrate them.

Mince the resins completely. Pound them together with the mortar and pestle or use a grinder. Add the remainder of the dry ingredients, and make an effort to pulverize them as completely as you can.

Add the tobacco, and continue to pound. Then add the Elegua oil a few drops at a time, up until you obtain a somewhat damp, crumbling, type of tacky blend.

Place this into a glass jar, allowing it age in a dark, cool place for approximately three weeks when it is ready to use.

Burn incense on a piece of a lit charcoal disc in a fire safe container.

You can burn incense for him every Monday.

Elegua Oil

Items Needed:
3 drops Avocado Oil
3 drops Coconut Oil
1 pinch of Sugar
1 pinch of Coffee Grounds
Eye Dropper Light Rum
Directions:
Mix all ingredients and blend into almond oil as a carrier. Use this oil to clear obstacles from your life and to create opportunities.

To Bring Change into Your Life with Oya

Items Needed:

9 Cans Sardines
9 Pennies
A Wick Cut in Nine Pieces
A Cloth with Colors
Corojo Butter or Palm Oil
Honey
Dark Wine
Container
Directions:

Place your image of Oya somewhere where she will not be disturbed. Open each can of sardine. Remove the sardine, placing them in a container. You do not need the sardines but you want to keep the oil with the cans. Add some Corojo butter or palm oil, honey and dark wine to each of the cans. Place the cloth where Oya is in setting the nine cans in front of her image. Place a penny in each of the cans and the wick. Light each wick it and petition to Oya for the change you desire.

To Petition Chango

Items Needed:
Cornmeal
Cut Okra
Corojo Butter or Palm Oil
Tomato Paste
Salt
6 Small Bowls
Directions:

Bring a pot of water to a boil and cook the cornmeal until it becomes thick. Remove from stove. Add the cut okras into the pot of cornmeal stirring well. Add tomato paste and a little bit of salt to taste. Lastly, add Corojo butter or palm oil and mix. Place back on the stove and bring back to a boil. Once everything is cooked, remove from stove and divide the mixture into your six bowls. Take these bowls to a park or any area where there are plenty of palm trees. Set each bowl at six different palm trees while petitioning to Chango. If you reside in an area that does not have palm trees, you can take them to a wooded area and leave all of them around a tall tree. Once you return home, light a candle for Chango.

Oshun Love Spell
Items Needed:
1 Pumpkin
Dominating Oil
Patchouli Oil
Come To Me Oil
Controlling Oil
Honey
Cinnamon Sticks
5 Fishing Hooks
5 Egg Yolks
1 Magnet
Beer
A Picture of the Person
Yellow Ribbon
5 Yellow Chime Candles
5 Copper Pennies (Pre 1982)
1 Seven Day Yellow Candle
Yellow Tablecloth
Perfume
*Optional: Paper bag
Directions:
Clean a space where you can set your spell so that it will not be interrupted. In the area, position a small table with a yellow tablecloth. Place on it an image or statue of Oshun. Set the yellow candle on the table and mist a little perfume.on it as a result when you call her spirit, she is pleased.

Cut the top open of the pumpkin and hollow out of all the inside and remove seeds. Position the magnet inside the pumpkin, next the picture of the person you desire inside of the pumpkin. If you do not have a photo of the person, you can replace it by writing their name on a paper bag. Attach the five fishing hooks on the picture or bag with name to the base of the pumpkin.

Recite as drop five drops of oil into the pumpkin:

With the dominating oil, I dominate you

With the patchouli oil, I seduce you

With come to me oil, I bring you to me

With controlling oil, I control your heart

Without breaking the yolks, place them inside the pumpkin, followed by the cinnamon sticks, honey and some beer. Once this is completed, set the top back on the pumpkin. Bind the yellow ribbon about the pumpkin and make five knots to close the spell. Light one yellow chime candle on top of the pumpkin, ringing the bell and make your request to Oshun what it is, precisely, that you want. For the next five days, continue to light the candles on top of the pumpkin. On the fifth day, take the pumpkin to the river and leave Oshun five copper pennies as a fee.

*I am going to say that I do not believe in controlling a person. What is meant to be will be. You know how Karma can be and I have felt it.

Pumpkin Pie for Oshun

Items Needed:

The Crust

1 1/4 cups All-Purpose Flour

1/4 cup Non-Salted Butter, melted or Solid Shortening, cold

1/4 cup of Iced Water

1/4 teaspoon Salt

Directions:

Make pie crust by combining the flour and salt. Cut the shortening into the flour/salt. Add the cold-water one tablespoon at a time. Mix dough and repeat up until the dough is moist enough to hold it together.

Form dough into a ball with your lightly floured hands. Using a lightly floured board, roll the dough out to about 1/8 inch thickness. With a sharp knife, cut dough 1 1/2 inch larger than a 9-inch pie pan turned upside-down. Roll the dough softly around the rolling pin and transfer it right side up onto the pie pan. Unroll, sliding dough into the bottom of the pie pan.

It is important to bake the crust for about 10 minutes using pie weights to keep the pie crust from puffing.

The Filling

2 Eggs

2 cups Steamed and Mashed Fresh Pumpkin

¾ cup Brown Sugar

1 ½ cup Evaporated Milk

2 tablespoons Melted Butter

½ teaspoon Salt

¾ teaspoon Cinnamon

½ teaspoon Ground Ginger

1/8 teaspoon Ground Nutmeg

Directions: Preheat oven to 400 degrees F.

Beat pumpkin in a large bowl with evaporated milk, eggs, brown sugar, cinnamon, nutmeg, ginger, and salt in a stand or electric mixer. Mix well, creating a smooth mixture. Pour into your readied crust. Bake for 40 minutes or until you can insert a toothpick in the center and it comes out clean.

Ochosi's Roasted Sweet Potato Fries

Items Needed:

3 medium sweet potatoes

Salt
Sugar
Palm oil
Paprika
Large bowl
Cookie sheet
Directions:
Preheat the oven to 450°F.

Peel sweet potatoes, cutting the ends off. Next, cut them into wedge shapes about the size of dinner fries. Place these in a large bowl and season them with salt, a pinch of sugar, palm oil and paprika. Toss them using your hands to be sure they are lightly coated with the oil and the flavorings. Spread the sweet potato wedges out on a cookie sheet in a single layer. Bake them in the oven for 25 to 30 minutes, turning them over halfway through the cooking time. Remove them from the oven and let them cool. Place them in a large bowl and give them to Ochosi as a cooked offering. Remove sweet potatoes after a suitable amount of time and get rid of them in natural surroundings as decided by means of insight.

Yemaya's Sweet Three Milk Cake
Items Needed:
2 cups Whole Milk
1 1/2 cups All-Purpose Flour
2 cups White Sugar (split as 1 cup and 1 cup)
1 teaspoon Baking Powder
1/2 cup Margarine or Unsalted Butter
5 eggs
1 ½ teaspoon Vanilla Extract (split as 1 teaspoon and ½ teaspoon)
1 14 ounces can Sweetened Condensed Milk
1 12 ounces can Evaporated Milk
1 1/2 cups Heavy Whipping Cream

9x13 inch Baking Pan
Baking Spray
Directions:
Preheat oven to 350 degrees F.

Grease and flour your 9x13 inch baking pan. Sift flour and baking powder together and set aside. Cream margarine or butter and one cup sugar together until fluffy. Add the eggs and the 1/2 teaspoon vanilla extract. Beat the mixture well.

Add the flour mixture to your butter mixture 2 tablespoons at a time; mix until well blended. Pour batter into a prepared sprayed pan. Bake at 350 degrees F for 30 minutes. Prick cake a number of times with a fork.

Combine the margarine, whole milk, and evaporated milk together. Pour over the top of the cooled cake.

Whip the whipping cream, the remaining 1 cup of the sugar, and the leftover teaspoon vanilla together until thick and spread on the top of the cake. Be certain to keep the cake refrigerated.

Oshun's Butternut Squash Soup

Items Needed:
3 cups Peeled and Cubed Butternut Squash
2 cups Chicken Broth
1/2 Minced Vidalia Onion
2 tablespoon Margarine or Butter
1/4 cup Cream
1/4 cup Applesauce
1/2 teaspoon Onion Powder
1/2 teaspoon Parsley
1/4 teaspoon Ground Sage
Pinch Ground Cinnamon
Pinch Ground Nutmeg
Salt and Pepper to taste
2 Sauce Pans

Garnish
Pumpkin Seeds or Sunflower Seeds
Sage Sprig
Directions:
Melt butter in a saucepan over low heat. Place minced onion in a pan and simmer until they start to lose their color. In the other pan, put in butternut squash and cover it with water. Bring to a boil and cook until the butternut squash is soft and tender. Drain, mash then add it to a pan with onions. Add applesauce, chicken broth, and the spices. Combine completely and to simmer continuously over low heat for about ten minutes, stirring from time to time. Take away from heat, mixing in cream, and add salt and pepper to taste. Serve with pumpkin seeds or sunflower seeds and a sprig of sage as a garnish.

Ogun's Creamy Potato Pork Chops

Items Needed:
6 pork chops
1 20 ounces package Frozen Hash Brown Potatoes, thawed
1 10.75 ounces can Condense Cream of Celery Soup
1 1/2 cups French Fried Onions, to be divided
1 cup Shredded Cheddar cheese, to be divided
1/2 cup Milk
1/2 cup Sour Cream
1 tablespoon Vegetable Oil
Salt and Pepper to taste
Large Skillet
Medium Bowl
9x13 inch Baking Dish
Directions:
Preheat oven to 350 degrees F.
In a large skillet, heat oil over medium-high heat. Add

pork chops and sauté until browned. Remove from skillet and place on paper towel to drain.

Mix in a medium bowl, condensed soup, sour cream, milk, salt, and pepper. Stir in potatoes, 1/2 cup onions, and 1/2 cup cheese. Combine and spread the mixture on the bottom of baking dish. Position pork chops over the potato mixture.

Cover the dish and bake for about 40 minutes, or up to inside temperature of the pork has reached 145 degrees F. Remove the cover; top with remaining onions and cheese then continue to bake uncovered for five more minutes.

Yemaya Coconut Fish

Items Needed:
1 pound Whitefish Fillets
1/2 cup Dry Bread Crumbs
1/4 cup Chopped Mixed Nuts
1/4 cup Shredded Coconut
1/4 cup Prepared Brown Mustard
1/4 cup Mayonnaise
1 teaspoon Granulated Sugar
1 teaspoon Salt
1/2 teaspoon Cayenne Pepper
Cooking Spray
Small Bowl
Medium bowl
Medium Baking Dish
Directions:
Preheat oven to 375 degrees F.

Lightly grease a medium baking dish. Mix brown mustard and mayonnaise in a small bowl. Mix in a medium bowl, shredded coconut, chopped mixed nuts, dry breadcrumbs, cayenne pepper, sugar, and salt.

Dip fish in the mustard mixture in the small bowl, followed by the breadcrumb mixture in the medium bowl. Position coated fish fillets in the prepared medium baking dish. Bake for 20 minutes or until fish can be easily flaked with a fork.

Oshun Honey Pound Cake

Items Needed:

1 cup (2 sticks) Butter, softened

1 1/3 cups Sugar

1/4 cup Honey

5 large Eggs

2 teaspoons Vanilla Extract

1 3/4 cups Flour, sifted

1 teaspoon Baking Powder

1/2 teaspoon Salt

Directions:

Preheat oven to 325 degrees F.

Lightly oil a 6-cup loaf pan. Beat the butter, sugar, and honey together using a mixer set on high until very light and fluffy--about 3 minutes. Beat in the eggs, one at a time. Add the vanilla extract. Add the flour, baking powder, and salt and beat until smooth.

Spoon into the prepared pan and bake until a skewer inserted into the center of the cake comes out clean--about 1 hour. Cool 15 minutes before unmolding.

TEN

Orishas in the Home

Altars or shrines are set up for several of reasons. They can take up a corner of an area or large enough to take up an entire room. It can be outdoors or small enough to fit into your bag, backpack or your pocket. They can be decked out with items and décor or informally decorated, boasting simple mainstays, flowers and candles. It is your belief that can bring your altar together. Your belief in what is not seen or heard. Setting up an altar is a means to develop your belief. It presents you with a physical space to go to focus yourself and concentrate on your spirituality.

You are establishing a commitment when you set up an altar to nurture and increase the connection you have encouraged between yourself and your beliefs. The initial step in creating your altar is determined on its purpose. Meditate before launching on your progress to establish your altar on these questions. Think about the parts of your spirituality or belief that speak to you deeply. Which god or gods do you notice yourself drawn to? What facets of your life would you like to change or develop?

If you do not have an altar to be used only for work with

the Ancestors, each Orisha should have a place in your home. Here are some suggestions:

Elegua: Behind Front Door
Yemaya: Living Rooms
Oshun: Kitchen, Bedroom
Chango: Fireplace Business Desk
Obatala: Living Room
Ogun: Behind Front Door
Oya: Library, Office

ELEVEN

Orishas Days Through The Week

Everyday Offerings

For the purpose of everyday rituals, you should have a candle holder, an incense burner, and a cauldron or pot, if possible. Additionally, some may choose to include a platform or stand for small blood sacrifices. If this is some that you cannot handle, it's okay. Just do the best that you can. It is all right to be not only original, but also imaginative so long as you keep to various etiquettes.

Typically offer to Elegua first except for blood offerings. Unless it is a blood tribute, Elegua is to be satisfied first because he clears the path for us to communicate to and be spoken to by other divinities and spirits. If you do not go through him first, you may misinterpret what is being expressed to you, or you may open yourself to harm or deceit by beings that focus in illusion. Opening up to the spirit world without Elegua makes you exposed. This is something you do not want to ignore.

Although any day is a suitable day to stay in contact with any Orisha, some days have a distinct feel to them, and these have an emotional impact on the way we make contact with. It furthermore helps to remember all of the Orishas you know of if you have a plan for daily practices. The way they have practiced well over hundreds of years has survived the ordeal of time in keeping people aware and getting things completed.

Different areas and groups have different days of the week they believe to be best. If your beliefs have a different agenda, you should adhere to that unless it feels wrong to you or if an Orisha has directed you to modify the day for your own practice. Some beliefs also have a monthly plan or lunar schedule.

Below, you will find a typical weekly schedule for your use.

Sundays: Obatala, Orunmila

Mondays: Elegua, Exu, Eshu, Ochosi

Tuesdays: Ogun, Ochosi

Wednesdays: Ogun, Babalu-Aye, Ochosi

Thursdays: Obatala, Orunmila, Ifa, Orula, Oldumare, Olofin, Olorun

Fridays: Chango, Oya, Oba, Babalu-Aye

Saturdays: Yemaya, Oshun

Conclusion

These beliefs, customs, and practices have stood the test of time. They have been shaped and molded by individuals from across the world. Including those from America, Brazil, Cuba, and Haiti, and have been incorporated with other religions such as Catholicism.

The beauty of this following is that it has survived for hundreds of years in other countries, away from its roots in Africa. Though so much has changed since then, the religion still remains intact.

In Haiti, the Yoruba people's beliefs, mixed with the Fon, serve as the foundation for Voodoo. Cubans call the beliefs Lucumi, "friend" in the Yoruba language. Religions and beliefs have also traveled as far as Brazil, known as Candomble or Macumba. It has even found new roots in Los Angeles, where it is known as Santeria, "worship of saints" in Spanish.

Though there are many colorful Orishas, the Yoruba still affiliate with one supreme being or God who created the universe. It was the Orisha whom God entrusted to look after the Earth and its inhabitants.

References

Brandon, G. (n.d.). Oshun. Encyclopedia Britannica. https://www.britannica.com/topic/Oshun

Changó. (n.d.) About Santeria. https://www.aboutsanteria.com/changoacute.html

Eleguá/Eshu. (n.d.). About Santeria. https://www.aboutsanteria.com/eleguaacuteeshu.html

Eshu. (n.d.). Encyclopedia Britannica. https://www.britannica.com/topic/Eshu

Mitchell, R. (1988, February 7). Power of the Orishas: Santeria, an ancient religion from Nigeria, is making its presence felt in Los Angeles. Los Angeles Times. https://www.latimes.com/archives/la-xpm-1988-02-07-tm-40762-story.html

Obatalá, Owner of All Heads. (n.d.). About Santeria. https://www.aboutsanteria.com/obatalaacute.html

Ochún. (n.d.). About Santeria. https://www.aboutsanteria.com/ochuacuten.html

Ogun. (2002, September 24). Wikipedia, the free encyclopedia. https://en.wikipedia.org/wiki/Ogun

Ogun. (n.d.). About Santeria. https://www.aboutsanteria.com/oguacuten.html

References

Oshun. (n.d.). Encyclopedia Britannica. https://www.britannica.com/topic/Oshun

Oyá. (n.d.). About Santeria. https://www.aboutsanteria.com/oyaacute.html

Santeria deities. (n.d.). BBC - Home. https://www.bbc.co.uk/religion/religions/santeria/beliefs/orishas.shtml

Yemayá. (n.d.). About Santeria. https://www.aboutsanteria.com/yemayaacute.html

Yemoja. (2002, October 4). Wikipedia, the free encyclopedia. https://en.wikipedia.org/wiki/Yem%E1%BB%8Dja

About the Author

Monique Joiner Siedlak is a writer, witch, and warrior on a mission to awaken people to their greatest potential through the power of storytelling infused with mysticism, modern paganism, and new age spirituality. At the young age of 12, she began rigorously studying the fascinating philosophy of Wicca. By the time she was 20, she was self-initiated into the craft, and hasn't looked back ever since. To this day, she has authored over 40 books pertaining to the magick and mysteries of life.

To find out more about Monique Joiner Siedlak artistically, spiritually, and personally, feel free to visit her **official website**.

www.mojosiedlak.com

facebook.com/mojosiedlak

twitter.com/mojosiedlak

instagram.com/mojosiedlak

pinterest.com/mojosiedlak

bookbub.com/authors/monique-joiner-siedlak

Other Books by Monique Joiner Siedlak

Practical Magick

Wiccan Basics

Candle Magick

Wiccan Spells

Love Spells

Abundance Spells

Personal Growth and Development

Creative Visualization

Astral Projection for Beginners

Meditation for Beginners

Manifesting With the Law of Attraction

Reiki for Beginners

The Yoga Collective

Yoga for Beginners

Yoga for Stress

Yoga for Back Pain

Yoga for Weight Loss

Yoga for Flexibility

Yoga for Advanced Beginners

Yoga for Fitness

Yoga for Runners

Yoga for Energy

Yoga for Your Sex Life

Yoga: To Beat Depression and Anxiety

Yoga for Menstruation

A Natural Beautiful You

Creating Your Own Body Butter

Creating Your Own Body Scrub

Creating Your Own Body Spray

THANK YOU FOR READING MY BOOK! I REALLY APPRECIATE ALL OF YOUR FEEDBACK AND I LOVE TO HEAR WHAT YOU HAVE TO SAY. PLEASE LEAVE YOUR REVIEW AT YOUR FAVORITE RETAILER!